Knowledge Books and Software

I am the Colour Ochre Warrior,

I stand so tall and proud.

Sometimes I feel strong,

And sometimes I feel down.

Knowledge Books and Software

Knowledge Books and Software

I call on my Spirits to guide me,

To guide me through my pain.

Spirits like Rainbow Serpent,

To help me find my way.

Knowledge Books and Software

Look at my colours.

All working as one.

They have a purpose.

To get things done!

Knowledge Books and Software

My colours have beauty.

And express different feelings.

I use these colours

As part of my healing.

Knowledge Books and Software

9

Look in the water,

Or just look around.

Knowledge Books and Software

Knowledge Books and Software

Colours underfoot,

Embedded in the ground.

Knowledge Books and Software

Ochres of Reds and Yellows,

Ochres of White and Blue,

Ochres of Green and Pink,

Ochres of Purple too!

Knowledge Books and Software

15

Ochre along the riverbank,

And even along the range.

So many ochre colours

That you can mix and change.

16

Knowledge Books and Software

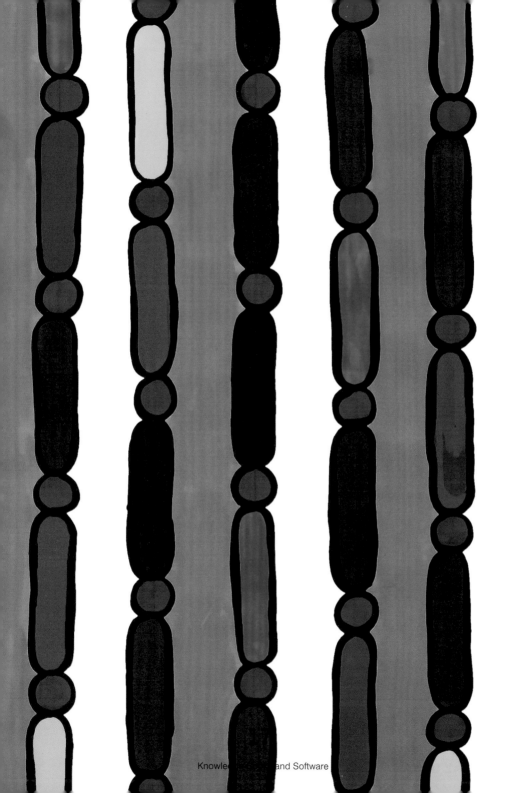

Thank you, Rainbow Serpent,

For sharing your special gift.

Colours to express my feelings,

Like Red to give me a lift!

Knowledge Books and Software

Knowledge Books Software

But today I will wear Green,

As I need to nurture and grow,

Like my leafy rainforest home,

Where beauty and nature glow.

Knowledge Books and Software

21

I am the Colour Ochre Warrior.

I say it LOUD and PROUD!

I yell it to the top of my lungs

And up into the clouds.

Knowledge Books and Software

Word bank

Ochre

Warrior

Spirits

guide

Rainbow Serpent

purpose

beauty

express

different

underfoot

embedded

special

nurture

rainforest

Knowledge Books and Software